Acadia
National Park

by Grace Hansen

Abdo
NATIONAL PARKS
Kids

Abdo Kids Jumbo is an Imprint of Abdo Kids
abdobooks.com

abdobooks.com

Published by Abdo Kids, a division of ABDO, P.O. Box 398166, Minneapolis, Minnesota 55439.
Copyright © 2019 by Abdo Consulting Group, Inc. International copyrights reserved in all countries.
No part of this book may be reproduced in any form without written permission from the publisher.
Abdo Kids Jumbo™ is a trademark and logo of Abdo Kids.

102018

012019

 THIS BOOK CONTAINS
RECYCLED MATERIALS

Photo Credits: Alamy, Getty Images, iStock, Minden Pictures, National Park Service

Production Contributors: Teddy Borth, Jennie Forsberg, Grace Hansen

Design Contributors: Dorothy Toth, Laura Mitchell

Library of Congress Control Number: 2018946057

Publisher's Cataloging-in-Publication Data

Names: Hansen, Grace, author.

Title: Acadia National Park / by Grace Hansen.

Description: Minneapolis, Minnesota : Abdo Kids, 2019 | Series: National parks
     Includes glossary, index and online resources (page 24).

Identifiers: ISBN 9781532182051 (lib. bdg.) | ISBN 9781532183034 (ebook) |
     ISBN 9781532183522 (Read-to-me ebook)

Subjects: LCSH: Acadia National Park (Me.)--Juvenile literature. | National parks
     and reserves--Juvenile literature. | Sieur de Monts National Monument (Me.)--
     Juvenile literature. | United States--Juvenile literature.

Classification: DDC 974.145--dc23

Table of Contents

Acadia National Park

Acadia National Park is in Maine. It was made a national monument in 1916 by President Woodrow Wilson. Three years later it became a national park.

5

At just under 50,000 acres (20,234 ha), Acadia is a smaller national park. Still, it is packed with beautiful natural features, plants, and animals.

Nature & Natural Features

More than 40 **mammal** species live in the park. Smaller mammals are more common. River otters and beavers can be found in ponds and lakes.

Porcupines and groundhogs often live in and near the forests. Spruce-fir forests are the most common in Acadia.

11

The park has lots of wild flowers. Asters and goldenrods are native to Acadia. They bloom in August and September.

13

Acadia also has beautiful **geological** features. Cadillac Mountain is within the park. Its highest point is 1,530 feet (466 m).

15

Other rock formations are nesting sites to peregrine falcons. These birds are **endangered**.

Wetlands make up more than 20% of Acadia. Rhodora is a flowering **shrub**. It can be found near the park's **marshes**.

With miles of coastline, saltwater animals also thrive. **Invertebrates**, like northern sea stars, can be found near the shore.

Fun Activities

Go tidepooling at low tide to see plants, rocks, and creatures

Kayak on Eagle Lake

Visit in autumn to see the beautiful fall colors

Watch climbers take on the pink-granite cliffs

Glossary

endangered – a species of plant or animal that is in danger of dying off.

geological – relating to the study of earth's physical structure and what its made of.

invertebrate – an animal that does not have a backbone or skeleton inside its body.

mammal – a warm-blooded animal with fur or hair on its skin and a skeleton inside its body.

marsh – a low, wet area, often thick with tall grasses.

shrub – a plant with woody stems that branch out close to the ground.

23

Index

Abdo Kids ONLINE

FREE! ONLINE MULTIMEDIA RESOURCES

Visit **abdokids.com** and use this code to access crafts, games, videos, and more!

Abdo Kids Code:
NAK2051